FAILURE IS NOT AN OPTION

LEARN HOW TO OVERCOME THE FEAR OF FAILING

By Patricia A Carlisle

Introduction

I want to thank you and congratulate you for choosing the book, *"FAILURE IS NOT AN OPTION: Learn How to Overcome the Fear of Failing"*.

This book contains proven steps and strategies on how to overcome the fear of failing.

When a person becomes unsuccessful and makes efforts at achieving something, but that thing eludes him, then that circumstance can cause a "let down". Anything that is not successful can only be regarded as a failure.

When a person makes a futile attempt at something he desires or is assigned a task and he fails to deliver, that is failure on the person's part. It can happen to anyone, it can also happen even to a bigger organization. But we cannot talk about failure without mentioning the fear that goes before failure.

Thanks again for choosing this book, I hope you enjoy it!

Patricia A. Carlisle, MSW, CBT

Patricia Carlisle- A Master Social Worker and a Cognitive Behavioral Therapist (CBT) gives out an expression of how important it is for an individual to take into consideration the concept of self-assessment to know what human, technical and conceptual skills they posses to perform or to achieve what they desire, or to deal with everyday life. However, every particular group of people has their own unique set of ideas, traditions and events including the frame of mind according to which people perform but there are many who faces problems and fail to maintain a healthy mind set affecting their behaviors and performance to those around them.

People like Patricia Carlisle are among those who have felt this urge of serving people and helping them out of their mental crisis towards a healthy life. She has experienced some close encounters in her personal life regarding mental health issues in her family and friends that has encouraged her to pursue this as her career.

Currently Patricia Carlisle is serving as a Certified On-Line Cognitive Behavioral Therapist with an extensive 15years of experience using Cognitive-Behavior Therapy Techniques. She envisions a world where everyone gets mental health treatment with no mental health stigma and to make it real she has already set up her own Holistic Measure Online Comprehensive Behavioral Healthcare Company after retiring from The Nord Center in The Partial Hospitalization Program (PHP) Dept for 5 years and Murtis H. Taylor Mental Health Center as a mental health counselor, psychological support technician and case manager for 10 years to emulsify her skills more professionally. Along with this, she has wrote down her passion as a clinician in 25 or more short books to help individuals and families get their life back, freeing them of the restraints of negative thinking, anxiety and depression by using different approaches. She is highly appreciated among her clients for her flexibility and professionalism of dealing with them graciously.

To reach her, make use of her direct website address: http://therapist2013.wix.com/e-therapy . As she is ready to inspire hope and contribute to health and well-being by providing the best online health care through comprehensive practice, education and research.

TABLE OF CONTENT

Chapter 1

FEAR

Fear has always been the greatest enemy of man when it comes to conviction. The mindset is very important in this aspect, many people have fallen victim and have been slain on the change of fear. People who are very good at manipulations make use of the fear factor to overcome opponents by instilling fear in them; some people make use of "mind games".

When a person uses mind-games technique to intimidate his opponent, and if the opponent begins to become afraid of the mastermind, then the battle is won even before the commencement of the war. When a person is afraid of something then that thing which he is afraid of will end up consuming them.

From the popular saying that "**cowards die a thousand times before they are being killed**" is so because a coward is being intimidated to believe that he lacks the ability to fight back, and many times the result is always that they are unable to stand up to challenges that comes their way. Some people are daring in life, they are not afraid to take the risk, and mostly, these categories of people always become successful simple because they decided to take the bull by the horn, and handle the situation decisively without fear.

It is advisable to be a bold person in life, the option of fear should not be entertained at all by any person who wishes to be successful in life. Life itself is adventure, we all come into this world to live, and one day we shall all depart this world. But that doesn't mean that we should leave before our time because of fear. No! That should not be so.

Chapter 2

WHAT IS THE FEAR OF FAILING

The fear of failing is when an individual's mindset is filled with anxiety of the possibility of not being able to attain success for whatever situation, or the person is not sure of what they are doing, or find themselves in. When the person begins to entertain panic or trepidation, that person has the fear of failing in him or her.

The fear of failing can be found in many areas of life's endeavor, for instance, the fear of failure is common among students who are writing exams, it is also common among married people, some are afraid of having a failed marriage because of the shame that such may cause them, and sometimes we notice that children who are from broken homes always have the fear of not suffering similar faith as their parents did in their marriage.

Business organizations are not exempted, business owners, entrepreneurs, companies etc. always want to be successful in business, when capital investment are made, it is expected that such expenditures will yield interest at the end of the fiscal year, but if the reverse is the case, a business may find it very difficult to continue to stay alive to continue to do business.

It is also common among sports men and women, those in the tract and field games, national teams, and many sports club, the fear of not being successful at competitions and during league games. There is always the anticipation of making a successful journey through the many games they have to play throughout the season, the fiscal year.

Chapter 3

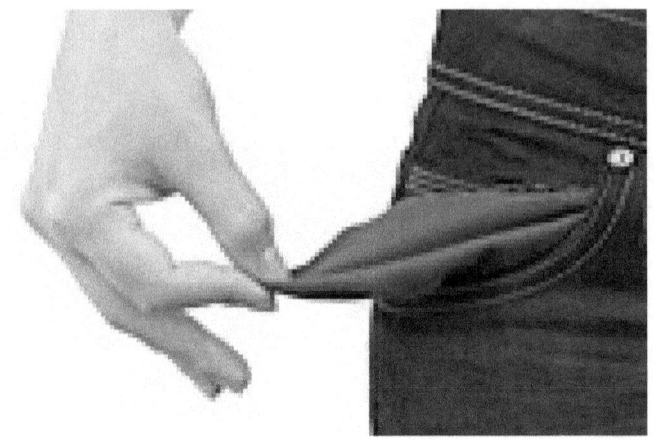

THE FEAR OF FAILURE CAN BE COSTLY

The fear of failure can be very costly, it could make the spirit of a person to be down-casted, and lead to loss of inspiration and expectation. The intimidated person may not be able to stand up to challenges when he is faced with one. The fearful person becomes easily intimidation, and may gradually drift into oblivion when he is being attacked by a dominant problem.

Hence, the fear of failure should not be optional for any individual or organization. The exact opposite of the fear of failure should be something that can make the mindset to think positively about success, in that way a person can develop into a very strong and courageous individual.

Chapter 4

EVERY FAILED ATTEMPT BRINGS NEW OPPORTUNITY

This is not to say that failure is not part of life, No! Life is not beds of roses, at some point in our lives, we may experience failures, this does not mean we should "drop dead", rather when we fail to achieve something, we try again, there is no harm in failure because **"failure is only a postponed success"** that is the kind of mindset recovery of after failing, that we should possess.

A lot of great scientist, and people in various areas of life only become successful after failed attempts at doing or achieving something, for instance, we have the man who is the brain behind the "electric bulb" Thomas Edison. Thomas Edison was the man who discovered and designed the electric bulb which was and still is, the foundation of the basic electric bulb manufacturing principle hitherto. He was able to achieve this after about nine hundred and ninety nine (999) failed attempts and he only became successful with the electric bulb invention when he tried it at the 1,000th time he attempted to design it. He made us to understand that every failed attempt brings new opportunity for a great achievement.

Before Abraham Lincoln became the President of the United States of America, he failed many times in his previous political ambition to take up leadership post. But did he give up? No! He did not give up. Michael Faraday also made several errors that resulted in failures when he embarked on projects and experiments that would assist him in generating electric current which is now the hall mark of the basic principle of electricity.

Today, he is the father of electric current and his theory is universal, and will ever be studied in the field of sciences. So to fail is not impossibility, and is not a new phenomenon under the sun. But, irrespective of that, failure should be seen as a "stepping stone" to achieving success. How then can we overcome the fear of failing when we are faced with responsibilities or challenges in life? The propositions in the next chapter will help us out as we read on.

Chapter 5

HOW TO OVERCOME THE FEAR OF FAILING

Embrace first Attempt:

Occasionally, we are faced with the fact that in certain circumstances and condition we find ourselves as a beginner, there is some form of anxiety over our ability to perform a particular task. Some of those occasions will be manifest in many areas of our daily endeavors ranging from academic responsibilities, family responsibilities, marriage responsibilities, business responsibilities, or work and office. The best bet for us is to embrace challenges in life.

That is the very first thing should come to mind, "**there is no harm in trying,**" as human beings we are not indispensable to errors, but it is not the man who cannot stand up to challenges that will succeed, but the man who is able to summon up the courage, and boldness to embrace first time attempt. What a person should have at the back of his mind is not outright success, but try to see what your efforts can yield, by putting in your very best, and see how far it goes. If you're successful, that will be fine, but if you are not, see failure as also another experience, so you learn from your experience, and make review of your lapses to see where you went wrong, and try again.

Embrace the pain:

Painful experience resulting from failures can be very devastating, but before the failure happens, have it in the back of your mind that whatever happens you will always be man enough or woman enough to embrace your failures, so in that way you will be able to challenge failure to its face and say to it **"I know you are waiting for me to fail, but guess what I will not give you the chance"** that is how to challenge failure to its face and "failure" will be humbled.

The Power of Positivity:

Positivity is when a person has the belief in a **POSITIVE POWER INHERENT IN THE HUMAN ABILITY,** yes! The power to generate internal energy that will spur an individual to succeed has been deposited in the heart and soul of ever man or woman. Those who are successful today in our world are those who dare to invoke their inner powers to the human base of reasoning, thinking, operation and intelligence; these people are able to explore the universe through their ability to believe in the power of positivism. In the recent, WWE tag team champions "NEW DAY" are not the best wrestlers, but they have this believe in the power of positivism and by this believe they are able to be successful and maintain their title. We see how their profile continues to grow by the day, they talk about it, they sing about it and they profess it to the whole world for anyone who cares to listen. Now! That is the power of positivity, you believe and you do not care what anybody else says, you do not care what opinion anybody else holds against you. All you care about should be that you have the power of positivity inside you, and this positive power will always defeat and overcome the negative powers going against your success.

Believe in Yourself

The man or woman who does not have faith in his or her ability and self is defeated naturally, and will end up being a failure. Why should you give in a failure? Whatever circumstances that you are in, make sure you believe in yourself. You are not someone else, and you should not try to be someone else, no way! You are only you, there is no another you, but you, so "beat your chest" and say I believe in myself. You are that special person that has no replicate; you are that person that God give talent that no one else has, there are no other you anywhere in the world but you. You exist in space and time, and where you are at a point in time is your "space and time". When you build your mind towards your potentials, failure will be scared of your new spirit of self supremacy. When you develop that supernatural power called believe in you, then be rest assured that failure will become jittery in your face.

Have Self Confidence

A person who wants to defeat must have self confidence, there are no two ways about it, and I'm not talking about pride, no! I am talking about self confidence which transcends from believe. When you already have that believe that you can do something that nothing can stop you. Then you need some level of self confidence. For instance, when you find yourself in a competition, where a price is to be won, you need to have confidence in yourself, it was when self confidence is establish you can be able to study your opponent's potentials, and discover his or her weakness, and take advantage of your competitors weaknesses by making your own potentials to dominate their weakness, then you can think of winning. But if your confidence level is below average or declining, you will have a very big problem competing with your opponent. "**A brave man is rattled by sudden attack**", but "**a man must be a lion to scare away his enemies**", and "**a man must be a fox to be able to identify traps**", these instances must be characteristics of a confident man or woman. If you lack these qualities, you are making yourself vulnerable to failure. A student needs to read his book if he or she ever wants to pass an examination, hence, as human beings there are certain attitude we need to build and develop if we ever want to overcome the fear of failing, and one of those characteristics is self confidence.

Having the Right Mind Set:

A person must be able to have the right mindset free from external influence. Yes! You must have your own mindset for every occasion in life. If you do not have your own mindset, you will be prone influence from those who are skilled at using the mind game to control your attention, distracting you, and making you not to have the focus that is required to become successful in life.

A person should have a unique mindset that is free from negativity and external influence. Don't allow someone to confuse you about the subject, or your attempt at something which you think you can do to make you successful. Some experiences in life shows that some people will try to bring you down, by telling you that you cannot make it, you don't have a chance, you are not fit for this job, you don't have the qualities or the talent, and so on and so forth. But every man has a talent, when you discover your own talent, and explore your own potentials you will definitely succeed in your efforts. But first, you must have the right mindset for you to be able to succeed in anything that you do. When you have it, then the fear of failing will only be history.

Avoid Living in Fear:

To some people, they cannot do anything but remain timid. It's quite unfortunate that so many people feel this way probably because of circumstances that has affected them, or the environment which they live in did not help them to develop properly, they become very afraid all their lives. This is wrong, we are not suppose to be afraid of anyone except **"GOD ALMIGHT"** not even the devil can intimidate us, because he has already been defeated over two thousand years ago. But the problem is more peculiar to people around poor environments in places like the Middle East, Africa, Asia, and some parts of other continents. Because of the constant exposure to poverty, suffering, terrorism, uprisings, wars, conflicts, economic crisis, insurgency, religious extremism, attacks, abuse, and various crimes, they become so timid that they continue to live in fear because their environment is not helping them at all. They are always being laid siege against and they have problems associated with security and uncertainties.

In some countries of the world, some locals are caught between cross fire and altercation between Government forces and Rebels, these locals continue to live in fear because the rebels always attack them. No matter what they do, the fear is always there. Even when normalcy return, these people suffer psychological trauma, and the after effects of civil war can be very devastating that rehabilitation can be very difficult to achieve. Many refugees around the world who are from conflict or troubled zones of the world are also not exempted, these people many continue to live in fear perpetually. But for those who environments are free from war, to avoid living in fear is an advice that should be taken seriously. The best bet is to live a simple and normal live in the community where you live. Avoid engaging yourself with gangs, cult groups, and also avoid associations with person of questionable character. Because some of them who are drug addicts or bullies can cause upset to a person by attacking a person if the individual does not cut the relationship with some of the guys who are gangsters.

Learn from the Mistakes of others:

A lot of people have made costly mistakes that led to their failures. Many of them ended up regretting their actions. You don't need to make the same mistakes, but you can learn from them to avoid being a failure, or to enable you overcome the fear of failing. For example, there are some sports men and women who have used drug enhancement performance in their careers. The consequences are that when they are investigated, and they are caught they are usually stripped of the title they have won, or banned from participating in any competition, and many times that could signify an end to a prospective career.

What made these sports men and women to engage themselves in drug enhancement performances? The reasons are not farfetched; they simply had "**the fear of failing**." They are afraid of losing the title, they want to win it by all cost, and they will do whatever it takes to win the trophy or prize. They are not willing to make that sacrifice required of a true champion, they want short cuts to success and this has led them to destroying their own career, how unfortunate for them, the shame, the stigma, and the tarnished image they have brought upon themselves always goes down to history books. You don't want to suffer similar fate I guess? Then if not, always try and do the right thing and the right time, learn from the mistakes of others, that is the right step in the right direction for successful people to avoid failures.

Early preparation:

Give enough time for preparation for anything that you are embarking on, whether you are preparing for exam, marriage, job interview, project, anything at all, always make sure you prepare adequately to avoid failing. Do not be taken by surprises. You will hear some people say "**I hate surprises**", when you are prepared, be alert about any unforeseen circumstances. That way, you will be in control of any situation.

Conclusion

Thank you again for choosing this book!

There are many avenues where the fear of failing can show up, the list is inexhaustible, but however, note that "**When a child falls down, he looks forward, but when an adult falls he looks backward to see what caused his down fall**", and "**the downfall of a man is not the end of this life**", but "**it could be the end of his life if he falls and refuses to rise again.**"

Definitely, failure is not an option; therefore we should always have the above principle as a yardstick or standard to keep up with situations that try to instill fear of failing in us. Serious efforts should be made to always rise to the occasion when challenged by circumstances that can warrant failing in our various endeavors.

Remember! Only successful people are always remembered, and their names are always written on the sands of time. Be among the successful people, but if you fail, learn from the experience and try again. Cheers!

Finally, if you enjoyed this book, would you be kind enough to leave a review for this book on Amazon? It'd be greatly appreciated!

Thank you and good luck!

Preview Of 'MINDSET: How you can become powerful and achieve success on your terms'

Chapter 1: WHAT IS MINDSET

Mindset is a simple idea discovered by a decade of research on achievement and success—a simple idea that makes all the difference.

In a fixed mindset, people believe their basic qualities, like their intelligence or talent, are simply fixed traits. They spend their time documenting their intelligence or talent instead of developing them. They also believe that talent alone creates success-without effort. They're wrong.

In a growth mindset, people believe that their most basic abilities can be developed through dedication and hard work-brains and talent are just the starting point. This view creates a love of learning and a resilience that is essential for great accomplishment. Virtually all great people have had these qualities.

Teaching a growth mindset creates motivation and productivity in the world of business, education, and sports. It enhances relationships

Go to Amazon.com to check out the rest of MINDSET: How You Can Become Powerful and Achieve Success on Your Terms

Check Out My Other Books

Below you'll find some of my other popular books that are popular on Amazon and Kindle as well. Alternatively, you can visit my author page on Amazon to see other work done by me. (https://amazon.com/author/patriciacarlisle)

A Guidance To Mental Training: Learn How To Develop Mental Resilience.

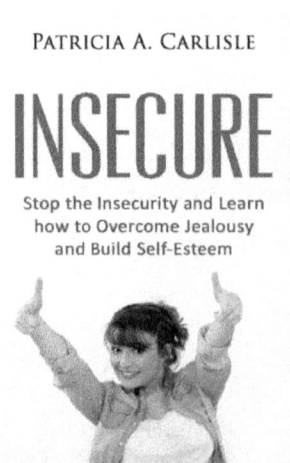

INSECURE: Stop the Insecurity and Learn how to Overcome Jealousy and Build Self-Esteem.

Letting Go: Learn How to Embrace the Future.

Over 600 Positive Affirmations That Will Change Your Life.

ANXIETY ATTACKS: You Could Be A Victim.

THE DEPRESSION CURE: How to Overcome Depression and Become Depression Free.

MINDFULNESS EXERCISES FOR BEGINNERS.

BONUS: SUBSCRIBE TO THE FREE BOOK

Beginners Guide to Yoga & Meditation

"Stressed out? Do You Feel Like The World Is Crashing Down Around You? Want To Take A Vacation That Will Relax Your Mind, Body And Spirit? Well this Easy To Read Step By Step

E-Book Makes It All Possible!"

Instructions on how to join our mailing list, and receive a free copy of "Yoga and Meditation" can be found in any of my Kindle eBooks.

NOTES

NOTES

NOTES

NOTES

NOTES

NOTES

NOTES

NOTES

NOTES

NOTES

www.ingramcontent.com/pod-product-compliance
Lightning Source LLC
Chambersburg PA
CBHW071017180526
45168CB00003B/1458